W9-CUX-998

THE BEST
DOGS
EVER

DACHSHUNDS
ARE THE
BEST!

Elaine Landau

⌐ LERNER PUBLICATIONS COMPANY · MINNEAPOLIS

To Loretta Dowell

Lerner Publications Company
A division of Lerner Publishing Group, Inc.
241 First Avenue North
Minneapolis, MN 55401 U.S.A.

Website address: www.lernerbooks.com

Library of Congress Cataloging-in-Publication Data

Landau, Elaine.
     Dachshunds are the best! / by Elaine Landau.
        p.   cm. — (The best dogs ever)
     Includes index.
     ISBN 978-1-58013-563-4 (lib. bdg : alk. paper)
     1. Dachshunds—Juvenile literature. I. Title.
     SF429.D25L36 2010
     636.753'8—dc22   2009013853

Manufactured in the United States of America
1 — BP — 12/15/09

J 636.753
LAN

TABLE OF CONTENTS

CHAPTER ONE

HOT DIGGITY DOG!

I'm thinking of a special dog. This dog is long on cuteness and style. It's long in other ways too. It has a long, low body. It also has long, floppy ears and a long snout.

Some call this canine cutie a wiener dog. It's also known as the hot dog hound. But it's really a dachshund—called a dachsie for short.

Quite a Hound

Dachsies are more than cute. They can be clownish and funny too. These dogs are also extremely sweet.

Dachshunds aren't timid either. At times, these little dogs can be bold, feisty, and tough. Put it all together, and you've got one really great pooch. Dachsies are a joy to be around.

DID YOU KNOW?

Dachshund is a German name. It's pronounced DAHKS-hunt. The dog's nickname—*dachsie*—is pronounced DAHKS-ee.

Same Dog, Different Look

Think you know what a dachsie looks like? You may be in for a surprise. Every dachshund has a long body, short legs, and a deep chest. Yet these dogs don't all look the same.

PICKING A NAME

What's a good name for a great dog that's long and low to the ground? See if any of these seem right for your new pet.

Lovey

Dash

Doxie

Skiddoo

Oscar

SCHNOODLE

Tootsie Roll

Sparky

Felix

Zeus

Dachsies come in two different sizes. The larger dogs are called standard dachshunds. They weigh up to 32 pounds (14 kilograms). That's about as much as three house cats.

The smaller dogs are called miniature dachshunds. They weigh 11 pounds (5 kg) or less. That's not much more than a newborn baby.

Standard dachshunds (*below, left*) are bigger than miniature dachshunds (*below, right*)—but they are still fairly small dogs.

Dachsies also have different coats. Some have short, smooth coats. Others are longhaired. They have long, silky hair on their ears, chest, legs, and tail.

The third type of dachshund coat is wirehaired. Such coats have a rougher feel to them. Wirehaired dachsies also have beards.

Smooth, wirehaired, and longhaired dachsies sit side by side in this photo.

Dachsies come in many colors too. Some are one solid color. Others are two different colors. Dachshunds can also have different patterns of color.

Most dachsie owners think their dogs are super. They love these alert, smart, and loyal hounds. They think dachshunds are the best dogs ever—and they could be right!

DOGS OF THE RICH AND FAMOUS

Some rich and famous people have owned dachshunds. These include the famous artist Pablo Picasso and the singer Madonna. Did you read the book *Charlotte's Web*? E. B. White wrote it. He had a dachshund too! In the photo below, E.B. White's dachshund, Minne, looks on as he works.

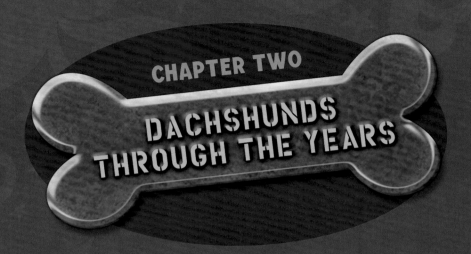

CHAPTER TWO
DACHSHUNDS THROUGH THE YEARS

Dachshunds first came from Germany. Early on, they were hunting dogs. They mostly hunted badgers. Badgers are animals that dig underground burrows.

A dachshund digs in the sand. Dachshunds' digging skills came in handy when they were hunting badgers in Germany.

In the 1700s, most people in Germany disliked badgers. Badgers dug up fields and lawns. They ate farm crops too.

This badger takes a break from digging.

German emperor Kaiser Wilhelm II (1859–1941, *left*) had dachshunds that he took with him when he traveled.

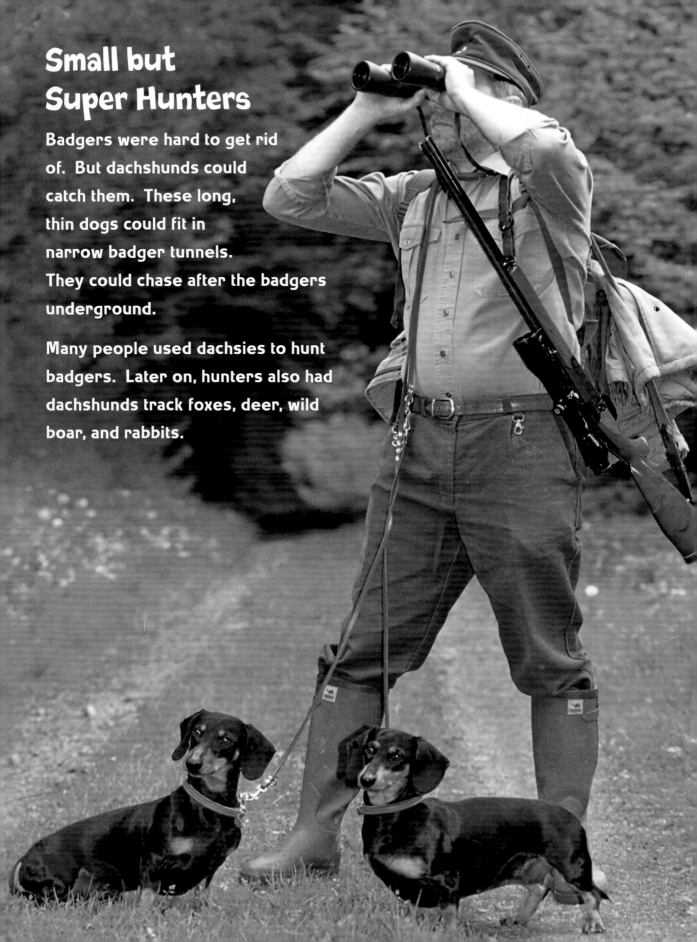

Small but Super Hunters

Badgers were hard to get rid of. But dachshunds could catch them. These long, thin dogs could fit in narrow badger tunnels. They could chase after the badgers underground.

Many people used dachsies to hunt badgers. Later on, hunters also had dachshunds track foxes, deer, wild boar, and rabbits.

HAPPY HUNTERS

Dachsies are still hunters at heart. They were bred for it. These dogs eagerly chase after squirrels in parks. They'll also follow the scent of gophers, chipmunks, and other animals.

In the late 1800s, many Germans began moving to the United States. Some brought their dachshunds with them. These little pooches soon became very popular. By the 1940s, dachshunds were among the United States' ten most popular dogs!

You Ain't Nothin' but a Hound Dog

These days, the American Kennel Club (AKC) groups dogs by breed. Some of the AKC's groups include the sporting group, the working group, and the toy group. Dachshunds are in the hound group.

Springer spaniels, like this one, are in the sporting group.

This boxer belongs to the working group.

Chihuahuas are in the toy group.

Dogs in the hound group do not look alike. Yet they have one thing in common: they are all fantastic hunters. Other dogs in this group are the beagle and the basset hound.

Beagles *(below)* and Afghan hounds *(left)* are in the hound group.

HELPING OTHERS

Some dachshunds work as therapy dogs. Therapy dogs are brought to hospitals or nursing homes. The patients there pet and play with the animals. The little dogs make the patients' days!

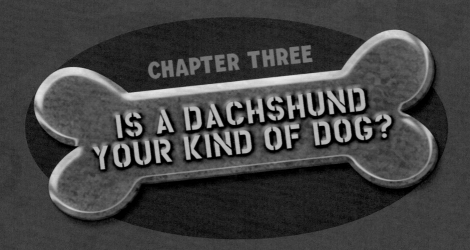

CHAPTER THREE

IS A DACHSHUND YOUR KIND OF DOG?

A dachshund is an appealing pooch. There's no doubt about that. Yet is it the right dog for you? Read on and decide for yourself.

Can You Dig a Dog That Digs?

One thing to know before getting a dachsie is that these dogs love to dig. They have been known to dig up yards and lawns. Inside, they may dig through stacks of toys, clean laundry, and magazines.

Some people don't mind a dog that digs. Others can't stand it. How do you and your family feel about it? Discuss this before bringing home a dachsie.

Easy to Exercise

Large dogs often need lots of daily exercise. You might spend hours hiking or jogging with a big German shepherd.

It's different with a dachshund. These dogs don't have to run through large open fields or go on all-day hikes. They'll do fine with a short daily walk. If you're dreaming of a dog that will run marathons with you, don't get a dachsie.

TOUGH TO TRAIN

Dachsies can be hard to train. They have minds of their own. You need lots of time, love, and patience to train one. After a while, your hard work will pay off.

A short walk through a park is plenty of exercise for a little dachshund.

Handle This Hound with Care

Dachsies must be treated gently. Their owners have to learn how to properly pick them up. A dachshund's back can easily be hurt. Some back injuries can damage your pet for life.

Do you have younger brothers and sisters who might play roughly with your dog? If so, pick another pet.

Do You Have Time to Spend with Your Dog?

Your dachsie will want to be with you. Are you busy most days after school?

Is your dog going to be alone most of the time?

Don't get a dachsie if this is the case. Bored and lonely dachsies often misbehave.

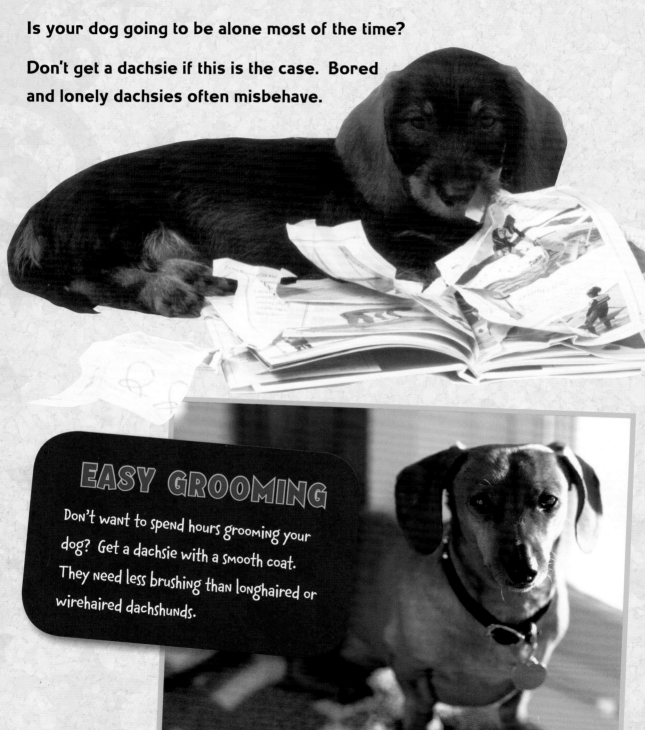

EASY GROOMING

Don't want to spend hours grooming your dog? Get a dachsie with a smooth coat. They need less brushing than longhaired or wirehaired dachshunds.

No dog is perfect for everyone. Maybe a dachshund is not for you. Yet if a dachsie is your kind of dog, you're lucky. This spunky little hound will delight you daily. Get set for a great time.

CHAPTER FOUR

A DACHSHUND OF YOUR OWN

So you've decided to get a dachshund. You've picked a great dog! Now you're about to bring your new pet home.

Have your camera ready. You'll want pictures. Be ready in other ways too. Have the things you'll need to help your dachsie settle in.

Not sure what you'll need to welcome Fido to your family?
This basic list is a great place to start:

- collar

- leash

- tags (for identification)

- dog food

- food and water bowls

- crates (one for when your
  pet travels by car and one
  for it to rest in at home)

- treats (to be used in training)

- toys

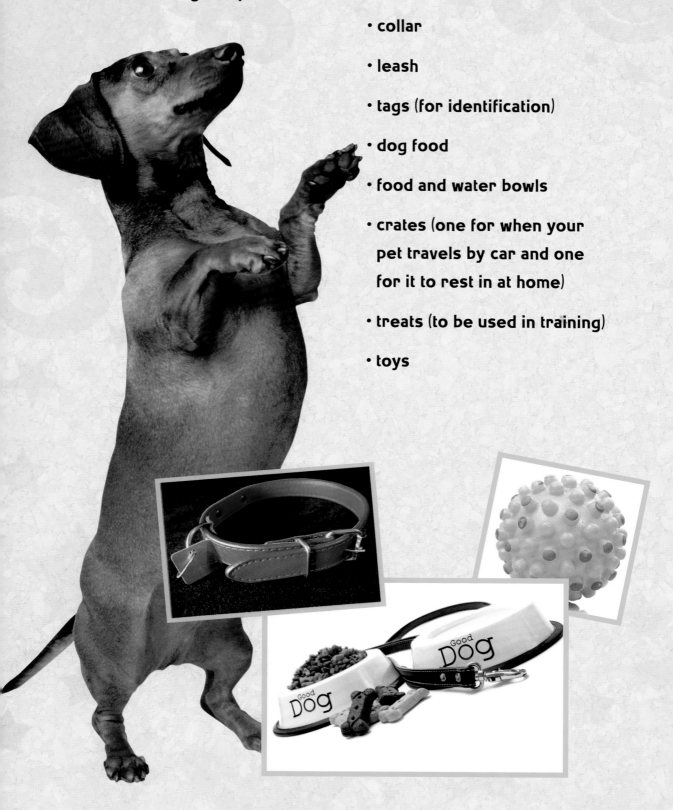

Keep Your Dog Healthy

You'll also want to take your dog to a veterinarian right away. That's a doctor who treats animals. They're called vets for short.

The vet will check your new pet's health. Your dog will also get the shots it needs.

A vet will help keep your dachsie in excellent health.

LONG LIVE DACHSHUNDS!

With good care, dachshunds can live a long time. Most will live from 12 to 18 years. At 10 years old, a dachshund is considered an older dog.

The vet is your dog's friend. Take your dachsie to the vet for regular checkups. Your dog should also see the vet if it becomes ill.

This dachsie feels at home in the water.

Yummy for the Tummy

A healthful diet is
important for your pet.
Feed your dachsie a
good-quality dog food.
Ask your vet which type
is best for your dog.

Do not be tempted to feed your dog table scraps. These tasty extras can cause your dog to gain weight. Being overweight can lead to back trouble in a dachshund.

SAFETY FIRST

Even dachshunds of NORMAL weight can have serious trouble with their backs. These little dogs NEED extra care to keep them in good health.

Don't let your dachshund jump down from a bed or couch. Jumping from this height can badly injure a dachshund's back. Many pet stores sell special steps to help short dogs get up and down. Make sure your dachsie has some.

Steps like these are specially designed to help little dogs climb up and down.

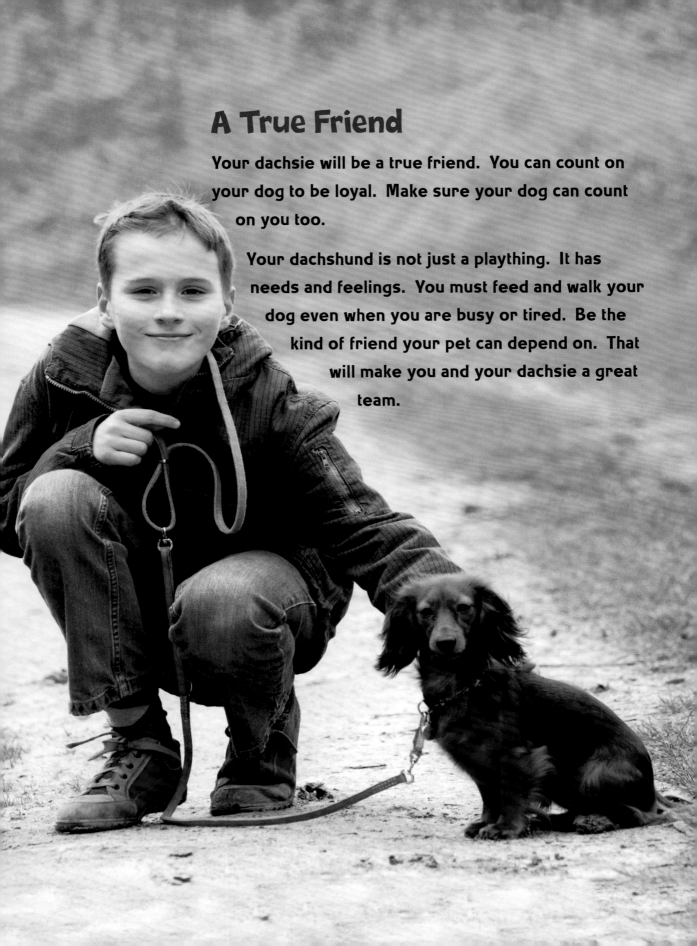

A True Friend

Your dachsie will be a true friend. You can count on your dog to be loyal. Make sure your dog can count on you too.

Your dachshund is not just a plaything. It has needs and feelings. You must feed and walk your dog even when you are busy or tired. Be the kind of friend your pet can depend on. That will make you and your dachsie a great team.

GLOSSARY

American Kennel Club (AKC): an organization that groups dogs by breed. The AKC also defines the characteristics of different breeds.

breed: a particular type of dog. Dogs of the same breed have the same body shape and general features. *Breed* can also refer to producing puppies.

canine: a dog, or having to do with dogs

coat: a dog's fur

diet: the food your dog eats

feisty: very lively or frisky

groom: to clean, brush, and trim a dog's coat

hound group: a group of dogs that have a good sense of smell and are often used for hunting

snout: the front part of a dog's head. It includes the nose, mouth, and jaws.

therapy dog: a dog brought to nursing homes or hospitals to comfort patients

veterinarian: a doctor who treats animals. Veterinarians are called vets for short.

FOR MORE INFORMATION

Books

Brecke, Nicole, and Patricia M. Stockland. *Dogs You Can Draw*. Minneapolis: Millbrook Press, 2010. In this book especially for dog lovers, Brecke and Stockland show how to draw many different types of dogs.

Gray, Susan H. *Dachshunds*. Mankato, MN: Child's World, 2008. Learn more about dachshunds in this fun and colorful title.

Landau, Elaine. *Your Pet Dog*. Rev. ed. New York: Children's Press, 2007. This book is a good guide for young people on choosing and caring for a dog.

Lunis, Natalie. *Dachshund: The Hot Dogger*. New York: Bearport, 2009. This title opens with a fun-filled dachshund race and goes on to reveal many facts about the "hot dog hound."

Stone, Lynn M. *Dachshunds*. Vero Beach, FL: Rourke, 2003. Stone offers an interesting introduction to dachshunds.

Websites

American Kennel Club

http://www.akc.org

Visit this website to find a complete listing of AKC-registered dog breeds, including the dachshund. The site also features fun printable activities for kids.

ASPCA Animaland

http://www2.aspca.org/site/PageServer?pagename=kids_pc_home

Check out this page for helpful hints on caring for a dog and other pets.

Index

Photo Acknowledgments

The images in this book are used with the permission of: backgrounds © iStockphoto.com/ Julie Fisher and © iStockphoto.com/Tomasz Adamczyk; © iStockphoto.com/Michael Balderas, p. 1; © iStockphoto.com/Alex Potemkin, pp. 4, 9 (top), 17; © Manzo Niikura/amana images/Getty Images, p. 5; © Tracy Morgan/Dorling Kindersley/Getty Images, pp. 6, 16, 20 (top), 23, 26-27; © Jeff Greenberg/Alamy, pp. 7 (top), 19 (top); © Jerry Young/Dorling Kindersley/Getty Images, p. 7 (bottom); © Yves Lanceau/NHPA/Photoshot, pp. 8-9; © New York Times Co./Hulton Archive/ Getty Images, p. 9 (bottom); © Juniors Bildarchiv/Alamy, p. 10; © Berndt Fischer/Photolibrary/ Getty Images, p. 11 (top); Private Collection/Ken Welsh/The Bridgeman Art Library, p. 11 (bottom); © Top-Pet-Pics/Alamy, p. 12; © age fotostock/SuperStock, p. 13; © GK Hart/Vikki Hart/Photodisc/ Getty Images, pp. 14 (top left), 24 (left); © Andrey Medvedev/Dreamstime.com, p. 14 (bottom left); © Jerry Shulman/SuperStock, p. 14 (right); © iStockphoto.com/Eric Isselée, pp. 14-15; © Susan Habermehl/Dreamstime.com, p. 15; © iStockphoto.com/YinYang, p. 18; © Yoshio Tomii/SuperStock, p. 19 (bottom); © Joe Polillio/Stone/Getty Images, p. 20 (bottom); © Maisie Paterson/Stone/Getty Images, p. 21 (top); © Andy Rain/CORBIS, p. 21 (bottom); © Sharon Montrose/The Image Bank/ Getty Images, p. 22; © Tammy Mcallister/Dreamstime.com, p. 24 (second from left); © April Turner/ Dreamstime.com, p. 24 (second from right); © iStockphoto.com/orix3, p. 24 (right); © Allison Michael Orenstein/Digital Vision/Getty Images, p. 25; © Everette Johnson, p. 26 (top);© Kazuhiro Nogi/AFP/ Getty Images, p. 26 (bottom); © Carsten Rehder/CORBIS, p. 27 (top); © Larry Reynolds/dogpix.com, p. 28; © blickwinkel/Alamy, p. 29.

Front Cover: © GK Hart/Vikki Hart/Photodisc/Getty Images.
Back Cover: © Tracy Morgan/Dorling Kindersley/Getty Images.